DUE

D1717049

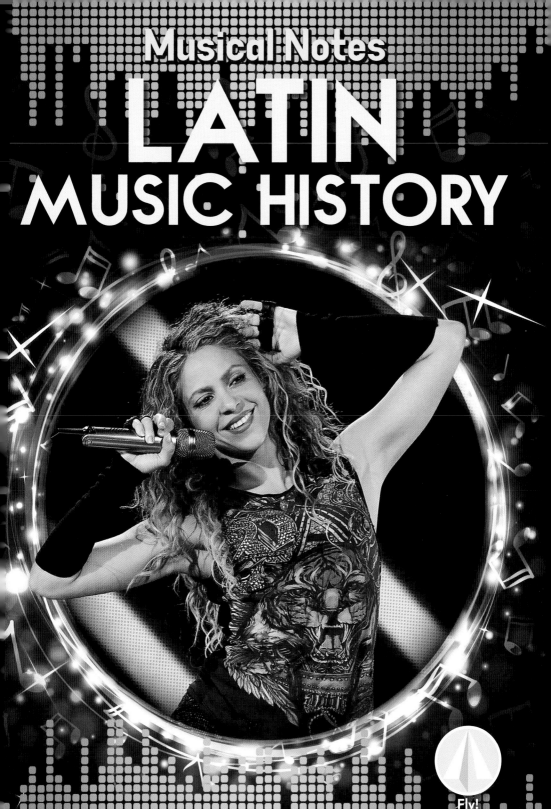

Musical Notes

LATIN
MUSIC HISTORY

Kenny Abdo

Fly!
An Imprint of Abdo Zoom
abdobooks.com

abdobooks.com

Published by Abdo Zoom, a division of ABDO, P.O. Box 398166, Minneapolis, Minnesota 55439. Copyright © 2020 by Abdo Consulting Group, Inc. International copyrights reserved in all countries. No part of this book may be reproduced in any form without written permission from the publisher. Fly!™ is a trademark and logo of Abdo Zoom.

Printed in the United States of America, North Mankato, Minnesota.
102019
012020

THIS BOOK CONTAINS
RECYCLED MATERIALS

Photo Credits: Alamy, AP Images, Getty Images, Shutterstock,
©livepict.com p.20 / CC BY-SA 3.0
Production Contributors: Kenny Abdo, Jennie Forsberg, Grace Hansen
Design Contributors: Dorothy Toth, Neil Klinepier

Library of Congress Control Number: 2019941329

Publisher's Cataloging-in-Publication Data

Names: Abdo, Kenny, author.
Title: Latin music history / by Kenny Abdo
Description: Minneapolis, Minnesota : Abdo Zoom, 2020 | Series: Musical notes |
    Includes online resources and index.
Identifiers: ISBN 9781532129421 (lib. bdg.) | ISBN 9781098220402 (ebook) |
    ISBN 9781098220891 (Read-to-Me ebook)
Subjects: LCSH: Latin American music--Juvenile literature. | Music and history-
    Juvenile literature. | Music--Latin American influences--Juvenile literature. |
    Dance music--Latin America--Juvenile Literature.
Classification: DDC 780.98--dc23

TABLE OF CONTENTS

LATIN MUSIC

Latin music is a mix of **culture** and tradition that created one of the most beloved music **genres** in the entire world.

Combining sounds and styles, Latin music has many **subgenres**. Salsa, Reggaeton, and Bachata are just a few.

7

OPENING ACT

Influences for the Latin **genre** can be traced back to **indigenous** music. The **Mayans** had a great interest in music. They invented many types of instruments like wind flutes and drums.

Lydia Mendoza was the first American-born Hispanic to record a Spanish song in 1928. She set the stage for other popular Latin musicians.

HEADLINER

Acts like Desi Arnaz, Carmen y Laura, and Tito Puente spiced up radio tunes with their own flare. Ritchie Valens' "La Bamba" was a big hit in 1958.

During the 1970s, Latin music began to mix with other American **genres**. Carlos Santana lit up the radio with his blend of Latin and psychedelic rock.

Selena made history in 1995. Her album *Dreaming of You* **debuted** at number one on the Billboard 200 chart. It was the first Spanish album to do so. She was portrayed by Jennifer Lopez in her **biopic** in 1997.

Julio Iglesias entered the Guinness World Records in 2013. He is the best-selling male Latin artist of all time. His son, Enrique, is the second highest selling Latin musician.

Today, Latin pop is enjoyed worldwide. Popular artists like Shakira, Ricky Martin, and Juanes top the charts with their energetic blend of tradition and **culture**.

GLOSSARY

biopic - a movie based on the life story of a celebrity.

culture - the customs, arts, language, and more of a nation or a group of people.

debut – a first appearance.

genre – a type of art, music, or literature.

indigenous - native to a certain place.

Maya - an ancient Indian people who lived in Central America and Mexico. The Mayan civilization flourished from about 250 to 900 CE.

subgenre – a more specific genre that is part of a larger genre.

ONLINE RESOURCES

Booklinks
NONFICTION NETWORK
FREE! ONLINE NONFICTION RESOURCES

To learn more about latin music history, please visit abdobooklinks.com or scan this QR code. These links are routinely monitored and updated to provide the most current information available.

INDEX